W0016973

ZAKIYA FATIN

ENTERPRISES

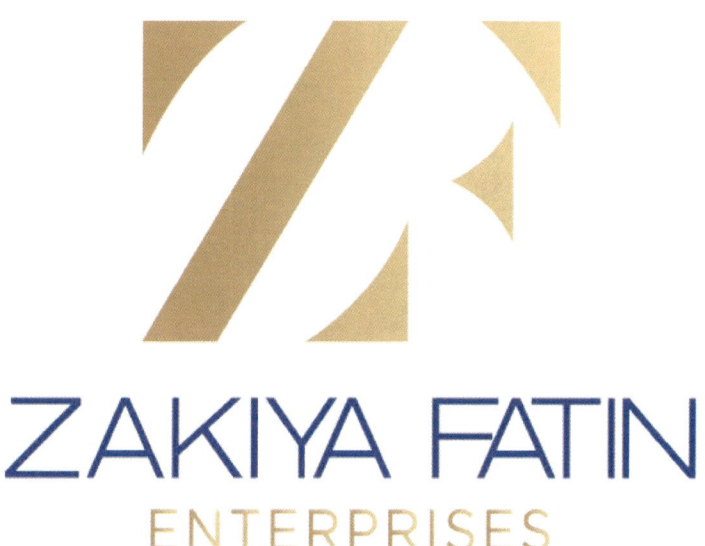

SIMPLE BOOK OF reminders for the YOUTH

WHAT MOST ADULTS WISH SOMEONE
TOLD THEM, WHEN THEY WERE YOUNG

ZAKIYA FATIN

Zakiya Fatin Enterprises

Copyright 2020 by Zakiya Fatin

All rights reserved, including the right of reproduction

In whole or in part in any form.

BOOK COVER DESIGN BY IRAM SHAHZADI

Manufactured in the United States of America

Library of Congress Cataloging-in- Publication Data

Fatin, Zakiya

Simple Book of Reminders for The Youth

What most adults wish someone told them when they were young / Zakiya Fatin

Print ISBN: 978-1-09834-405-4

eBook ISBN: 978-1-09834-406-1

*This book is dedicated to the little girl in me
and all the children who need these words and this insight, wisdom,
information, and advice.*

GUESS WHAT

As children, preteens, and young adults, there are so many things we go through, endure, and experience. These things can be confusing and hard, but can also be things that are often fun, liberating, and exciting, and sometimes, things that are hurtful, life changing, and unfair. This book of "Reminders" is filled with information, answers, encouragement, and things to remember as you journey and navigate through your life.

This book will give you clarity, guidance, and understanding, while reminding you, that you have the strength, courage, and drive to get through the situations, experiences, and things you may face. You may approach this book free to start from the place you feel called to begin. For example, you may open the book to Reminder 12, which may be the reminder that speaks to you, or applies to a feeling, situation, or circumstance of which you are facing or dealing. You should start there. Every day you open this book, you'll start with a new reminder—or maybe even the same reminder from the day before. If that is what you need, it will show up. Just open the book and trust that you'll open it to the exact page that you need for the day. You can even pray and ask for guidance, understanding, or make a simple request for help and trust that when you open the book, what you prayed for will be there.

Be sure to read slowly. Let each reminder you read sink in. Take your time. Read it two or three times if you need to. These reminders will speak to the wisdom of your soul. In many ways, the reminders will confirm some things you already know, some things from which you have been running from acknowledging or accepting about yourself or about your life. It is my hope that these reminders support you, lift you, encourage you, and give you a greater sense of self.

I could only imagine who I would be. What I would have done differently, or what things could I have avoided if I had access to the information contained in this book when I was young.

There are empty spaces on each page. Use them to write any feelings or thoughts you may have as you read and sit with each reminder.

Reminder #1

You can do and be anything you desire!

What will you do first? Who do you see yourself becoming?

_____

_____

_____

_____

_____

_____

_____

_____

_____

_____

_____

_____

_____

_____

_____

_____

Reminder #2

Ask for help when you need it! Silence won't get you the help you need!

Do you need help with something? What is it? Who can you ask for support?

_____

_____

_____

_____

_____

_____

_____

_____

_____

_____

_____

_____

_____

_____

_____

Reminder #3

Think positive thoughts even when you are feeling bad. What you focus on is what grows.

Don't give negativity power over you or how you feel.

What positive things can you focus on today? What good things are happening in your life?

_____

_____

_____

_____

_____

_____

_____

_____

_____

_____

_____

_____

_____

_____

_____

Reminder #4

Be kind to yourself, love yourself, trust yourself, and know that there is no one in this world that knows you better than you know yourself.

What are some kind and loving things you can do for yourself?

You know what you need better than anyone, trust yourself.

_____

_____

_____

_____

_____

_____

_____

_____

_____

_____

_____

_____

_____

_____

Reminder #5

Look in the mirror today. Look into your own eyes and say, "I love you!"

Did you do it? How did it make you feel?

_____

_____

_____

_____

_____

_____

_____

_____

_____

_____

_____

_____

_____

_____

_____

Reminder #6

Nothing is wrong with you! Everything about who you are is perfect! It's okay if you don't believe it right now. It's still true.

What do you believe about yourself?

_____

_____

_____

_____

_____

_____

_____

_____

_____

_____

_____

_____

_____

_____

_____

_____

_____

Reminder #7

Smile today! It is your smile that lights up the world!

What or who makes you smile? Why?

_____

_____

_____

_____

_____

_____

_____

_____

_____

_____

_____

_____

_____

_____

_____

_____

Reminder #8

Hard times build you up to become strong and wise! Don't let the hard times break you! You are stronger than you think. Keep your head up, young one!

How have you become stronger? How are you different and wiser from the things you've gone through?

_____

_____

_____

_____

_____

_____

_____

_____

_____

_____

_____

_____

_____

_____

_____

Reminder #9

Love and respect your parents and try not to judge them! They are doing the best they know how! Nobody taught them how to be parents.

"Nobody taught your parents how to be parents." What do you think about that? How does it feel to know that you are one of your parents greatest teachers?

Reminder #10

Have lots of fun and remember to play often. Don't take life so seriously!!

What are some of the things you can do for fun when things start to feel overwhelming?

_____

_____

_____

_____

_____

_____

_____

_____

_____

_____

_____

_____

_____

_____

_____

Reminder #11

Remember that everyone's life looks different. Don't think that just because someone has more material things than you, that they experience and are more loved and more fortunate

than you! They could have a lot of things and not experience the attention, time, love, and affection you receive.

Everyone is raised differently. How do you feel about how you are being raised?

_____

_____

_____

_____

_____

_____

_____

_____

_____

_____

_____

_____

_____

_____

Reminder #12

Keep going. You got this. Don't give up!

What keeps you going? What inspires you? What motivates you?

_____

_____

_____

_____

_____

_____

_____

_____

_____

_____

_____

_____

_____

_____

_____

_____

_____

Reminder #13

Don't change who you are to fit in with others! Who you are is enough!

What do you think would happen if you let your friends and family see you for who you really are?

_____

_____

_____

_____

_____

_____

_____

_____

_____

_____

_____

_____

_____

_____

_____

Reminder #14

You are who you are. Don't worry about what others say and think about you. Just be you!

You will find your power in staying true to who you are.

Who are you?

_____

_____

_____

_____

_____

_____

_____

_____

_____

_____

_____

_____

_____

_____

_____

Reminder #15

Dream big and go for it. Nothing can stop you but you!

What are your dreams? What are you passionate about?

_____

_____

_____

_____

_____

_____

_____

_____

_____

_____

_____

_____

_____

_____

_____

_____

_____

_____

Reminder #16

Your mind is powerful! What you allow yourself to believe in is what you have the ability to create!

What do you believe? What do you want to create?

_____

_____

_____

_____

_____

_____

_____

_____

_____

_____

_____

_____

_____

_____

_____

_____

_____

Reminder #17

Be honest and always tell the truth.

Is it easy or difficult for you to tell the truth? Why?

_____

_____

_____

_____

_____

_____

_____

_____

_____

_____

_____

_____

_____

_____

_____

_____

_____

_____

Reminder #18

Be brave and confident even when you feel afraid and doubtful! Push past the fear.

What would you allow yourself to do if fear didn't exist?

_____

_____

_____

_____

_____

_____

_____

_____

_____

_____

_____

_____

_____

_____

_____

_____

Reminder #19

Trust your instincts. They won't steer you in the wrong direction!

Do you trust yourself to always do what is best for you?

_____

_____

_____

_____

_____

_____

_____

_____

_____

_____

_____

_____

_____

_____

_____

_____

Reminder #20

Follow the path laid before you. It will take you to some amazing places! That means sometimes you have to step away from the crowd and do your own thing.

What does it look like to do your own thing?

_____

_____

_____

_____

_____

_____

_____

_____

_____

_____

_____

_____

_____

_____

_____

_____

Reminder #21

Put lots of effort and commitment into everything you do!

What does commitment mean to you? What are you committed to?

_____

_____

_____

_____

_____

_____

_____

_____

_____

_____

_____

_____

_____

_____

_____

_____

Reminder #22

If you start it, finish it! Even if you don't like it, complete it so you don't have to repeat it.

How many times have you had to start over because you didn't fully apply yourself?

_____

_____

_____

_____

_____

_____

_____

_____

_____

_____

_____

_____

_____

_____

Reminder #23

Make responsible choices! Think things all the way through.

Do you think before you act? Or do you just do things and worry about the consequences later?

_____

_____

_____

_____

_____

_____

_____

_____

_____

_____

_____

_____

_____

_____

_____

_____

Reminder #24

You can always change your mind about things. You are never stuck! You just have to have the courage.

What makes you feel stuck?

_____

_____

_____

_____

_____

_____

_____

_____

_____

_____

_____

_____

_____

_____

_____

_____

Reminder #25

It's okay to feel what you feel because how you feel matters. Just don't expect everyone to understand. Your experience is your experience and you are entitled to your own experience.

What are you feeling right now?

_____

_____

_____

_____

_____

_____

_____

_____

_____

_____

_____

_____

_____

_____

_____

_____

Reminder #26

You are not the negative things people think or say about you! You're not the negative things you say and think about yourself. Tell yourself the truth about who you are. I'm sure there are many things you can think of and have proof of that make you unique.

What makes you unique? What is your superpower?

_____

_____

_____

_____

_____

_____

_____

_____

_____

_____

_____

_____

_____

Reminder #27

People will always have opinions. Let them have their opinions. Just never let other people's beliefs make you question or forget who you are, or what you have the ability to create and do for yourself.

Sometimes you have to be willing to do things differently. You sometimes have to be the one who thinks outside of the box, the one who moves away from the crowd.

Are you that person?

_____

_____

_____

_____

_____

_____

_____

_____

_____

_____

_____

_____

_____

_____

Reminder #28

Cherish the good times and carry those memories with you forever!

Is there someone you miss? What would you say to them if they were sitting in front of you?

Reminder #29

Never stop believing in yourself! Possibilities are endless!

Do you believe anything is possible?

_____

_____

_____

_____

_____

_____

_____

_____

_____

_____

_____

_____

_____

_____

_____

_____

Reminder #30

Nothing can stop you but you! Keep going!

What will it take for you to keep going?

_____

_____

_____

_____

_____

_____

_____

_____

_____

_____

_____

_____

_____

_____

_____

_____

_____

Reminder #31

Stay Focused! Don't be distracted by the things that don't matter.

What or who are you allowing to distract you?

_____

_____

_____

_____

_____

_____

_____

_____

_____

_____

_____

_____

_____

_____

_____

_____

_____

_____

Reminder #32

Get excited about the future! It's yours to create now go be great!

What can you get excited about?

_____

_____

_____

_____

_____

_____

_____

_____

_____

_____

_____

_____

_____

_____

_____

_____

_____

Reminder #33

Be thankful for the things you have! Appreciate and honor them. Believe it or not, you are more fortunate than most.

Can you list some things you are grateful for?

_____

_____

_____

_____

_____

_____

_____

_____

_____

_____

_____

_____

_____

_____

_____

_____

_____

_____

Reminder #34

You matter! What you need matters! Who you are matters! What you believe in matters!

What you think matters! You matter!

What do you think you need, that you don't already have? Who do you think you need to become to be accepted or fit in?

_____

_____

_____

_____

_____

_____

_____

_____

_____

_____

_____

_____

_____

_____

_____

_____

Reminder #35

Be free! Be creative! Be bold! Be daring! Have fun in the process!

What does it feel like to be yourself? Would you feel free?

_____

_____

_____

_____

_____

_____

_____

_____

_____

_____

_____

_____

_____

_____

_____

_____

_____

Reminder #36

Never be afraid to explore new things, new ways, and new ideas! There is a whole world out there just waiting to be explored.

What do you want to explore? What new ideas do you have?

_____

_____

_____

_____

_____

_____

_____

_____

_____

_____

_____

_____

_____

_____

_____

_____

Reminder #37

Every time you tell yourself you can't, remind yourself you can, and move forward!

Sometimes all it takes is courage to move forward. Are you courageous enough to remain focused and keep moving no matter what?

_____

_____

_____

_____

_____

_____

_____

_____

_____

_____

_____

_____

_____

_____

_____

_____

Reminder #38

There is greatness inside of you. Don't be afraid to let the world see it! By showing them your greatness, you'll remind them that there is greatness inside of them too!!

What's inside of you that you hide from the world?

_____

_____

_____

_____

_____

_____

_____

_____

_____

_____

_____

_____

_____

_____

Reminder #39

Forgive the people that hurt you and move on! That doesn't mean they get to stay in your life and do the same thing over and over again. I'm saying you can forgive them and move on. The forgiveness piece is for you!

It takes more energy to stay mad at someone, than it does to let go and free yourself of the anger and hurt you've been carrying. Who do you need to forgive?

_____

_____

_____

_____

_____

_____

_____

_____

_____

_____

_____

_____

_____

_____

_____

_____

Reminder #40

Everyone isn't nice, but that doesn't mean you shouldn't be. Don't change who you are because of someone else's behavior.

What do you do when someone treats you badly? Do you blame yourself, and say it was your fault? Do tell yourself you must have done something to deserve bad treatment? Or do you excuse yourself from that person's presence, because you deserve better?

_____

_____

_____

_____

_____

_____

_____

_____

_____

_____

_____

_____

_____

_____

_____

Reminder #41

Change is hard sometimes and nothing stays the same. Remind yourself you can handle the changes that come your way.

What's changing in your life?

_____

_____

_____

_____

_____

_____

_____

_____

_____

_____

_____

_____

_____

_____

_____

_____

_____

Reminder #42

You are powerful and simply amazing! Don't you forget that!

How often do you forget how powerfully amazing you are, because your focus is on the negative things and the mistakes you've made?

_____

_____

_____

_____

_____

_____

_____

_____

_____

_____

_____

_____

_____

_____

_____

_____

Reminder #43

Not everyone is going to get or understand who you are. You may not even know or understand who you are yet, but that doesn't mean you should stop being you or exploring the things that make you, you! Just go with it, it will all make sense later!

What are some of the qualities and characteristics that make you, you?

_____

_____

_____

_____

_____

_____

_____

_____

_____

_____

_____

_____

_____

_____

Reminder #44

Make someone laugh today! Always invest in other people's happiness! You never know what someone else is going through.

What can you do to put a smile on someone's face today?

_____

_____

_____

_____

_____

_____

_____

_____

_____

_____

_____

_____

_____

_____

_____

_____

Reminder #45

Remember your innocence, even when people try to make you feel guilty!

You can forgive yourself; we all make mistakes. Why sit around and feel guilty? When you can feel better now.

_____

_____

_____

_____

_____

_____

_____

_____

_____

_____

_____

_____

_____

_____

_____

_____

_____

_____

Reminder #46

Sometimes hearing the truth hurts, but don't get angry about it. Embrace it and change your behavior if that is what is required.

What behavior do you need to change? What can you do better?

_____

_____

_____

_____

_____

_____

_____

_____

_____

_____

_____

_____

_____

_____

_____

Reminder #47

Don't skip steps or cut corners. You miss important details and lessons when you do.

Do you pay attention to details? Do you ask questions when things are not clear?

Reminder #48

No one knows what's inside your mind, what you're thinking, or how you feel. Find someone you can trust and talk to him. It doesn't feel good to keep things bottled up inside and it's not healthy to do so.

Do you keep things bottled up inside? What do you think would happen if you let it out and talked about it instead?

_____

_____

_____

_____

_____

_____

_____

_____

_____

_____

_____

_____

_____

_____

_____

_____

Reminder #49

Make sure you take time for you today. You don't always have to be busy or doing something. It's okay to spend time with yourself.

What special thing can you do for yourself toady?

_____

_____

_____

_____

_____

_____

_____

_____

_____

_____

_____

_____

_____

_____

_____

_____

Reminder #50

Think about what you want to do, think about who you want to be in life, and begin to explore what it will take to get there.

What are some steps you can take to reach your goals?

_____

_____

_____

_____

_____

_____

_____

_____

_____

_____

_____

_____

_____

_____

_____

_____

_____

Reminder #51

Show up and give one hundred percent of your very best in every area of your life! You get out what you put in.

How much work are you putting in? Are you getting results that match your efforts?

_____

_____

_____

_____

_____

_____

_____

_____

_____

_____

_____

_____

_____

_____

_____

_____

Reminder #52

You have a mind of your own. Make sure the decisions and choices you make, you make because it's what you want to do and because it's what's best for you! Don't allow people, situations or circumstances to force you into things that don't honor who you are. If it doesn't feel right, don't do it. Trust your gut.

Do you do what you know is best for you? Or do you allow others to convenience you to do something different?

_____

_____

_____

_____

_____

_____

_____

_____

_____

_____

_____

_____

_____

_____

Reminder #53

Keep things simple. Don't make it harder than it has to be!

Keep it simple.

Don't over think it.

How do you make things harder than they have to be?

_____

_____

_____

_____

_____

_____

_____

_____

_____

_____

_____

_____

_____

_____

_____

_____

Reminder #54

Be okay with who you are and what you have. Remember, it's perfectly okay to want more and to be more. Go after what you seek and don't allow anyone to tell you that you can't have it!

What are you seeking? What do you want for yourself?

_____

_____

_____

_____

_____

_____

_____

_____

_____

_____

_____

_____

_____

_____

_____

_____

_____

Reminder #55

You do not have to suffer in silence. If something is wrong, tell someone who can help. If things are happening that make you feel unsafe or uncomfortable, talk to someone you know and trust that someone will be able to support you. Don't be silent about it.

What do you need to talk about? Is there something you need to say or tell someone?

_____

_____

_____

_____

_____

_____

_____

_____

_____

_____

_____

_____

_____

_____

Reminder #56

Always keep your word—to yourself and to others. It's also okay to change your mind about things. Just make sure you communicate to others when you do.

Communication is important. Are you good at expressing yourself and telling others how you feel?

_____

_____

_____

_____

_____

_____

_____

_____

_____

_____

_____

_____

_____

_____

_____

_____

Reminder #57

Just in case you've never been told, you are important, you are loved, and your presence is necessary and needed.

How does it feel to know that you matter?

_____

_____

_____

_____

_____

_____

_____

_____

_____

_____

_____

_____

_____

_____

_____

_____

Reminder #58

What your parents go through is not your fault and it has nothing to do with you. It does affect you, but it's not on you.

Are you blaming yourself for something you think is your fault even though it isn't?

_____

_____

_____

_____

_____

_____

_____

_____

_____

_____

_____

_____

_____

_____

_____

_____

Reminder #59

Things happen in life that you may not understand. Somethings may hurt you, make you sad, or make you feel angry, or even feel afraid. Just know that you will overcome whatever it is. Don't let it change you in a negative way. Trust that things will be okay, and they will be.

Do you trust that everything will work out?

_____

_____

_____

_____

_____

_____

_____

_____

_____

_____

_____

_____

_____

_____

Reminder #60

Respect your parents and your elders. They have been here longer than you, which means they can teach you something.

What have you learned from your parents or an elder today?

_____

_____

_____

_____

_____

_____

_____

_____

_____

_____

_____

_____

_____

_____

_____

_____

Reminder #61

Life is not always about what you want. Sometimes you have to work for what you want.

Sometimes what you want will be given to you, and sometimes what you want is just not the best thing for you. In any case, be okay with the outcome.

What are you grateful for? Have you ever experienced a better outcome than you expected?

_____

_____

_____

_____

_____

_____

_____

_____

_____

_____

_____

_____

_____

_____

Reminder #62

Your parents need you as much as you need them, just in different ways. So make sure you are not just thinking about yourself. Think about what others may need as well.

Have you made a difference in the lives of others? How?

_____

_____

_____

_____

_____

_____

_____

_____

_____

_____

_____

_____

_____

_____

_____

_____

Reminder #63

It is okay to not be okay. You don't have to pretend to be if you're not.

Maybe writing down what's going on can help you.

_____

_____

_____

_____

_____

_____

_____

_____

_____

_____

_____

_____

_____

_____

_____

_____

Reminder #64

Everyone is not your friend. Trust what you feel.

How do you feel about some of the people you call your "friend"?

_____

_____

_____

_____

_____

_____

_____

_____

_____

_____

_____

_____

_____

_____

_____

_____

_____

_____

Reminder #65

It is okay to not know what to do, and its okay to not know what you're doing. Ask questions.

What questions can you ask?

_____

_____

_____

_____

_____

_____

_____

_____

_____

_____

_____

_____

_____

_____

_____

_____

_____

Reminder #66

Tears don't make you weak. Most of the time, it takes strength to cry and show emotion. Don't stifle your feelings. Express them out loud, or write them down.

You can write them down below.

_____

_____

_____

_____

_____

_____

_____

_____

_____

_____

_____

_____

_____

_____

_____

_____

Reminder #67

Pray for yourself, the things you want, and for other people too.

Do you pray? Are you praying for yourself and for others?

_____

_____

_____

_____

_____

_____

_____

_____

_____

_____

_____

_____

_____

_____

_____

_____

_____

_____

Reminder #68

Never judge people or situations based on what you see. If you don't have all the facts, what you think and believe or tell others could be way off.

Have you ever formed an opinion about someone or something without knowing all the facts or details?

_____

_____

_____

_____

_____

_____

_____

_____

_____

_____

_____

_____

_____

_____

_____

_____

Reminder #69

Your parents love you even if they don't know how to show it.

Can you think of some things your parents have done for you because they love you?

_____

_____

_____

_____

_____

_____

_____

_____

_____

_____

_____

_____

_____

_____

_____

_____

_____

Reminder #70

What you're going through may seem unfair. Everybody's life experiences are different and everyone deals differently with the things they go through. It is all designed to make you stronger, wiser, and better than you were yesterday. You'll see when you get to the other side of it.

You can write about it here for now if you need to.

_____

_____

_____

_____

_____

_____

_____

_____

_____

_____

_____

_____

_____

_____

Reminder #71

It is perfectly normal to be curious about your body and wanting to explore things as you get older. Ask your parents or your guardian for age appropriate things to look at.

What do you have questions about? Writing your questions down may make it easier to talk about with your parents or guardian.

_____

_____

_____

_____

_____

_____

_____

_____

_____

_____

_____

_____

_____

_____

_____

Reminder #72

It's okay to be a kid. Don't rush to be grown. Adults have responsibilities you're not even thinking about.

Are you ready to pay your own bills, and buy your own clothes? Are you ready to take on the responsibilities of an adult?

_____

_____

_____

_____

_____

_____

_____

_____

_____

_____

_____

_____

_____

_____

_____

_____

_____

Reminder #73

It doesn't have to be perfect. You don't have to be perfect to measure up! Just do the best you can.

Are you doing your best?

_____

_____

_____

_____

_____

_____

_____

_____

_____

_____

_____

_____

_____

_____

_____

_____

Reminder #74

Just because you struggle and have to work harder than others do, does not mean you're not smart or gifted. Your gifts and talents just look different than theirs.

What do you have to work hard at doing to be great?

_____

_____

_____

_____

_____

_____

_____

_____

_____

_____

_____

_____

_____

_____

_____

_____

_____

Reminder #75

Be proud of yourself! Even if others aren't.

Are you proud of yourself? If not, you should think of all the things you've made it through and overcome. That will make you proud.

_____

_____

_____

_____

_____

_____

_____

_____

_____

_____

_____

_____

_____

_____

_____

_____

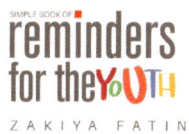

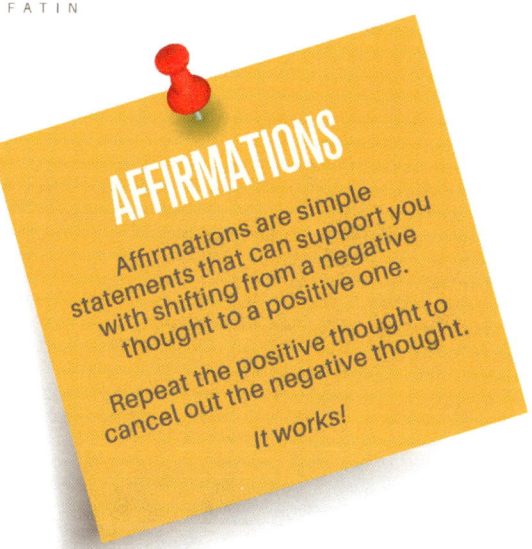

AFFIRMATIONS

Affirmations are simple statements that can support you with shifting from a negative thought to a positive one.

Repeat the positive thought to cancel out the negative thought.

It works!

SIMPLE BOOK OF
reminders
for the YOUTH
ZAKIYA FATIN

accept YOURSELF
My best is enough.

SIMPLE BOOK OF reminders for the YOUTH

ZAKIYA FATIN

love YOURSELF
I am love, loved, and lovable.

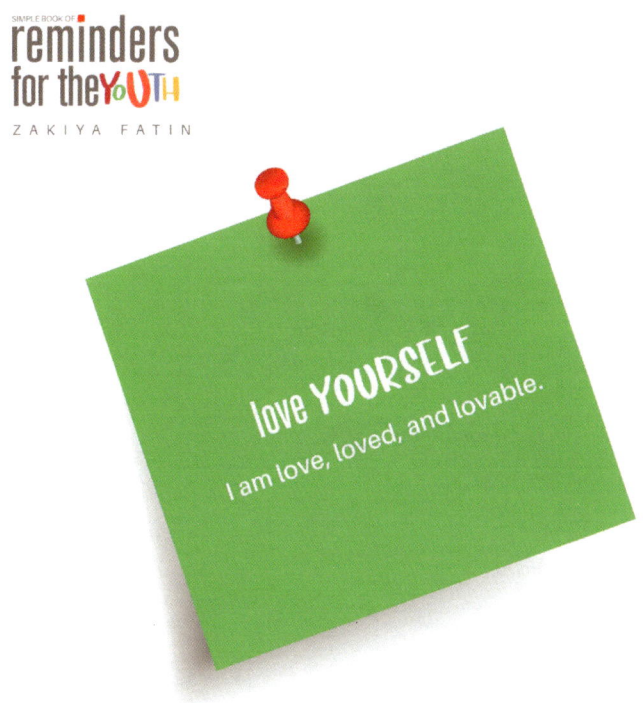

SIMPLE BOOK OF reminders for the YOUTH

ZAKIYA FATIN

be YOURSELF
Everything I want to do, I can do.
I am the creator of my reality.

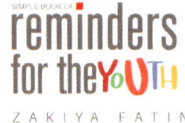

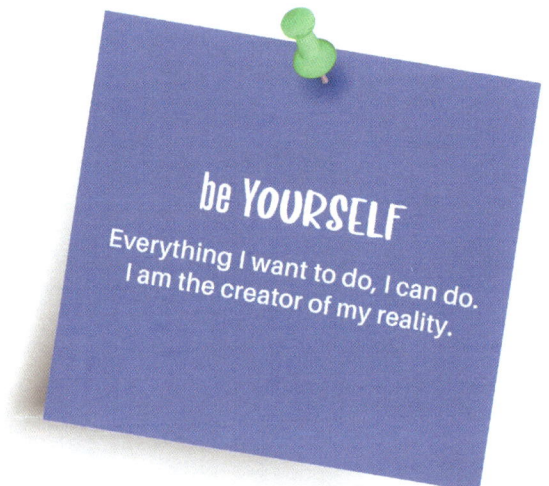

SIMPLE BOOK OF
reminders
for the YOUTH
ZAKIYA FATIN

trust YOURSELF

Everything I want, need, and desire comes to me easily and effortlessly.

NOTE FROM THE AUTHOR

Never stop believing in yourself. Always follow your dreams and never let a mistake stop you from trying a second, third, fourth or fifth time to get it right. Keep going you've got this!

Find something every day to be grateful for and do the things that make you proud to be who you are.